Level 4
Budding Reader

Book 1: Reading four and five-letter "a" words

Amanda Riccetti

Illustrations by Steven Gomez

Library of Congress Control Number: 2019917923
Published in the United States by Kindle Direct Publishing,
an Amazon Comany, Seattle, WA.
www.kdp.amazon.com
www.readingwithmissamanda.com

Big City Publishing is a registered trademark of Big City Montessori School.
Library of Congress Cataloging-in-Publication Data

Riccetti, Amanda, 2019 —
Reading with Miss Amanda, Level 4: Beginning Reader—Book 1: Reading four and five-letter "a" words
Written by Amanda Riccetti; Illustrations/Graphic Design by Steven Gomez,
Design Concept by Robert Riccetti, Edited by Kimberly Lopez
p. cm.
Summary: In the Level 4 Blue Series, Miss Amanda uses phonetic learning
to practice reading four and five-letter words and a short story.
ISBN-13: 978-1-950675-30-2 | ISBN-10: 1-950675-30-0

Printed in the United States of America

This book is dedicated to every child who wants to learn how to read and the adult in their life who wants to support them.

Contents

What to Expect

PHONETIC LEARNING: Throughout this series, children learn letter sound recognition. In the Montessori Method, we do not call letters "ABC" but rather refer to their sound. Use the phonetic letter sounds listed below to become familiar with the way the sounds will be written throughout the books. Remember to always call letters by their sounds.

PHONETIC LETTER SOUNDS: a- ah, b- buh, c- ck, d- duh, e- eh, f- Fff, g- guh, h- Hhh, i- ih, j- juh, k- ck, l- Lll, m- Mmm, n- Nnn, o- oh, p- /p/, q- kwa, r- Rrr, s- Sss, t- /t/, u- uh, v- Vvv, w- wuh, x- ks, y- yuh, z- Zzz

INTUITIVE LESSONS: The lessons in the *Reading with Miss Amanda* series will feel completely intuitive to children, even if they have different styles of learning. The illustrations and games help to engage younger children at the beginning, then evolve into appealing exercises that will teach your child to read.

TIME SPENT: Expect to spend about 10-20 minutes per day on the book for five days a week. Each book could take as little as one week to master or up to two months, depending on the pace of the child and the level the child is on.

REPETITION IS GOOD: Children love repetition, and it drives learning. For example, the popular book *Goodnight Moon* by Margaret Wise Brown might bore an adult, but children love the repetition of phrases. So if you use this book and think, "that's repetitive," remember — it is designed that way.

Reading with Miss Amanda

5 levels

	Typical Age*	Reading Level**	Example
L 1	3+ Pre-Reader	Has not learned letter sounds yet	"ah," "buh," "ck"
L 2	4+ Becoming a Reader	Has not learned to phonetically read three-letter words yet	"Max," "rat," "cat"
L 3	4+ Beginning Reader	Has not learned to read short sentences yet	"The crab ran and hid."
L 4	4+ Budding Reader	Has not learned to read four or five-letter words in short sentences yet	"The crab ran on the sand."
L 5	5+ Advanced Reader	Has not learned silent vowels (cake) or blended vowels (oo, ai) yet	"The cook baked a cake."

*The ages listed are merely guidelines that Montessori teachers use as a basis to introduce reading lessons.

**This series is also ideal for older children who need to learn reading or children with a learning difference, such as dyslexia.

If you have any issues, go to the FAQs at the end of the book.

Hi there! Welcome back to my class! In this book you will find lessons that will help you learn to read. Practice makes permanent.
Come join me!

mask

Lesson 1
Reading and Matching

Tip

If your child comes across a letter they have forgotten, read the sound and continue. Through repetition, your child will learn the letters.

Remember that you can stop at the end of any lesson and can repeat or restart a lesson at any time. Just follow your child's natural pace!

Extension Lesson

This book offers "extension lessons" to help your child further experience the concepts of the lessons. The extension lessons are only for children who can form letters.

In this lesson, you will read a word aloud and point to the corresponding picture that matches.

Let's get started!

grass

glass

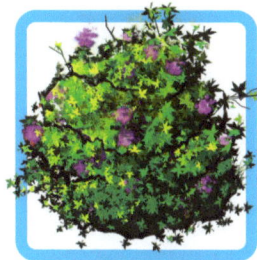

8

lamp

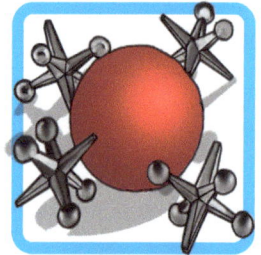

9

plant

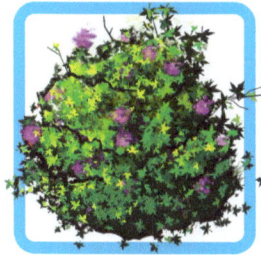

mask

11

jacks

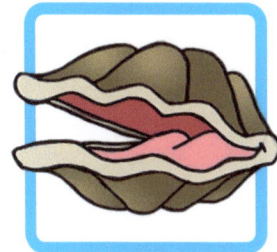

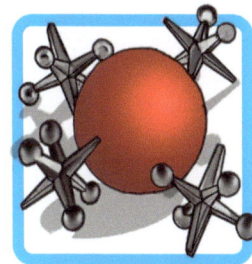

clam

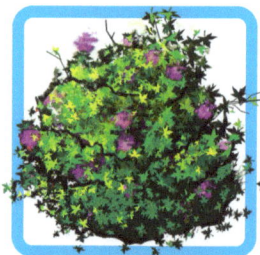

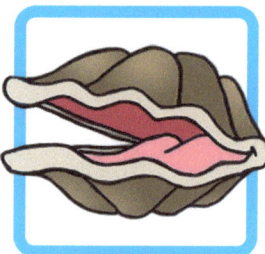

stamp

You reached your goal!

Lesson 2
Reading Cards

Tip

Have your child place their finger under each letter as they sound out the letters. For example, "ck-ah-/t/, cat." Then have your child read the word.

Extension Lesson

Dictate this lesson to your child. When dictating, use letter sounds only. Remember, it's good practice to stretch out the middle sound so your child can hear it clearly. For example, "Please spell ck-aaaah-/t/, cat." For some children, it's helpful to provide a red and blue pencil.

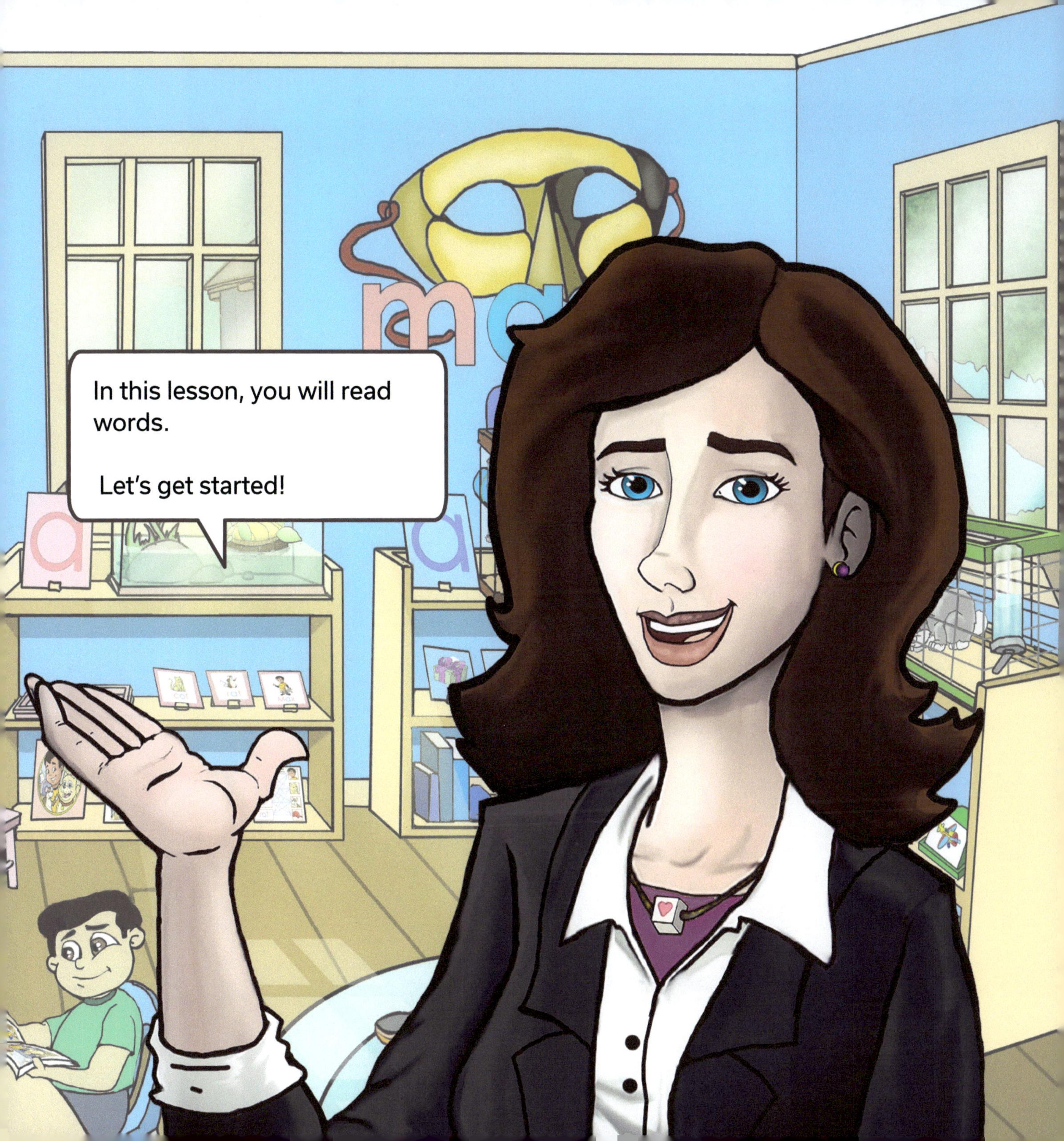
In this lesson, you will read words.
Let's get started!

camp

hand

18

sand

land

snap

clam

plant

slam

grass

mask

stamp

glass

You reached your goal!

✋ Stop

In order to maintain your child's interest in the task and ability to continue learning, you will need to follow their pace. "Stop" pages are a reminder to offer your child a break, an extension lesson, or to continue on with the next lesson.

- Read Option A if you think it is time for a break, Option B if you are offering an extension writing lesson, or Option C if you are continuing.

- When you offer an extension lesson after a lesson, it's good practice to STOP for the day and start the next lesson another day. The extension lessons are only for children who can form letters.

- It is common for children to forget something they have just learned, so when you return, review the past lesson before starting the next one. Remember, it's a marathon, not a race.

A. You really stuck it out. Time to take a break.
I look forward to our next lesson together.
See you soon!
B. Nice work!
One more lesson before I go. Please get some paper. Now, it's time for a dictation lesson. Practice makes permanent.
C. Nice work!
Let's continue.

Lesson 3
Reading a Word List

Tip

Have your child place their finger under each word as they go down the list. If your child has any questions about the definition of a word, feel free to stop and describe the word's meaning.

Extension Lesson

Have your child copy one of the word lists, and draw a picture for one of the words. After they finish, have your child read the words back to you.

In this lesson, you will read words in a list.

Let's get started!

crab

plan

camp

hand

plant

land

lamp

pants

scrap

sand

ramp

band

grass

glass

naps

jacks

scan

slam

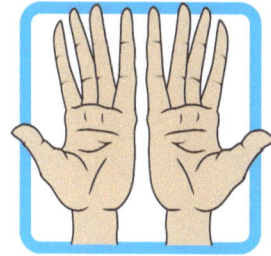

hands

clam

clamp

snap

slap

stand

A. You really stuck it out. Time to take a break.
I look forward to our next lesson together.
See you soon!
B. Nice work!
One more lesson before I go. Please get some paper. Now, it's time for a dictation lesson. Practice makes permanent.
C. Nice work!
Let's continue.

Lesson 4
Reading Short Sentences

Tip

Have your child read one word at a time while moving their finger under each letter. Then, read the sentence slowly while moving their finger under each word. Read the same sentence until your child can string the words together. With practice, your child will read sentences.

Feel free to explain English-language rules as they come up.For example: "Mommy, why does the word 'rat' have an 's' at the end?" "Well, when there is more than one rat, you add an 's' at the end."

Extension Lesson

Have your child copy a sentence and draw a picture to go with it. After they finish, have your child read the sentence back to you.

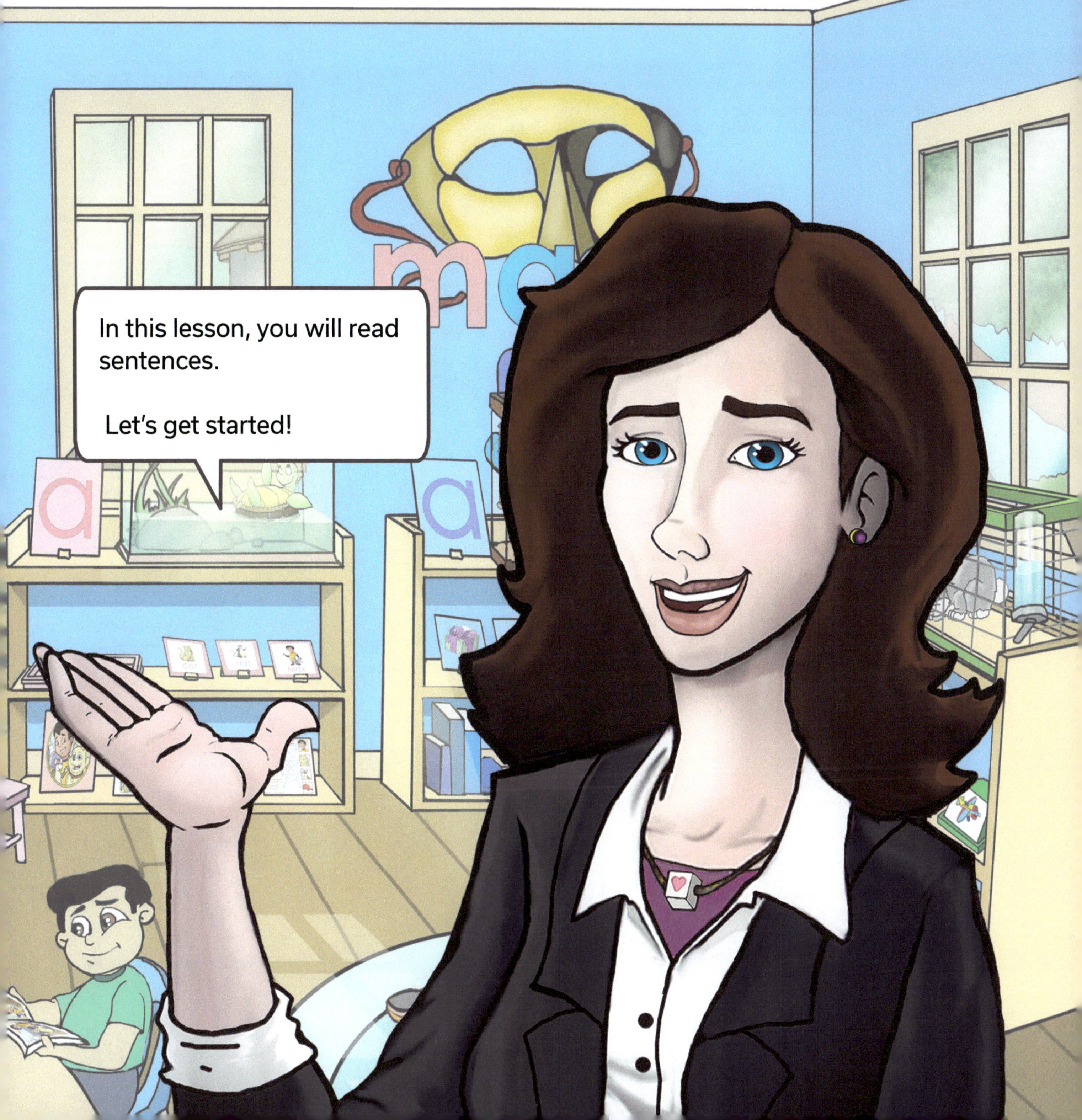
In this lesson, you will read sentences.
Let's get started!

The stag ran fast.

The clam is in the sand.

The bell rang and rang.

The hand can snap.

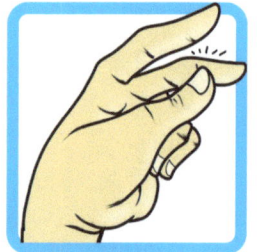

The plant is in her hand.

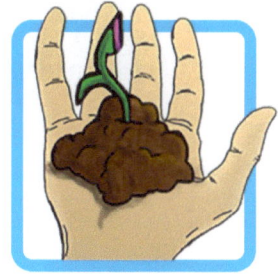

The lamp is on the stand.

The crab ran on the sand.

The ant stands on the plant.

A. You really stuck it out. Time to take a break.
I look forward to our next lesson together.
See you soon!
B. Nice work!
One more lesson before I go. Please get some paper. Now it's time for a dictation lesson. Practice makes permanent.
C. Nice work!
Let's continue.

Lesson 5
Reading a Short Story

Tip

Have your child read by tracking the words with their finger. If your child struggles, make immediate corrections and have them read the sentence more than once. Repetition drives learning.

Extension Lesson

Children love reading about themselves. Write short sentences with your child's name, pet's name, friends, etc., and make personal books.

The Crab in the Sand
by Amanda Riccetti

There is a land of
plants and sand.

The plants stand
grand in the sand.

In the sand sat a clam.

A crab swam to the land.

The clam snapped at the crab.

The crab ran fast to the grass.

He hid flat in the sand.

The crab can relax at last.

Just for fun, can you find four crabs, two clams, a mask, and the jacks?

Have fun looking! See you soon!

mask

DO NOT TURN THIS PAGE
UNLESS YOUR CHILD HAS
MASTERED THIS BOOK.

Great Job!

Congratulations!

You reached your goal. You completed Blue Book 1. This golden coin is for you. Keep up the hard work, and I look forward to seeing you in the next book!

Accomplishments

The stamp is a symbol of your hard work. When you complete stamps for all the levels, you will be an advanced reader.

L1

Book 1   Book 2   Book 3   Book 4   Book 5

L2

Book 1   Book 2   Book 3   Book 4   Book 5

L3

Book 1   Book 2   Book 3   Book 4   Book 5

L4

Book 1   Book 2   Book 3   Book 4   Book 5

L5

FAQ

? How much time should I spend on the book?

- Daily repetition is the best way to learn new information. If you skip days, you may end up repeating past lessons.

- An ideal schedule would be at least five times a week for about 20 minutes per session.

? Do I have to read the whole book?

- No. You can stop at the end of any lesson and restart at any time.

- You can also restart at any point in the book depending on how well your child has grasped each lesson.

? Is it okay to skip a section?

Yes. If your child has mastered a section, keep working on the other sections that are still challenging.

? What should I do when my child completes a lesson?

FOLLOW THE CHILD — Ask your child if they would like to have another lesson. If they say you can continue, this indicates your child is still interested and enjoying their time with you.

? When is my child ready for the next book?

In the back of this book are word lists that you can review before advancing to the next book. When your child can read the words and the short story with ease, they are ready to advance to the next book. Remember, this is a marathon, not a race.

? What are the four core skills my child needs to learn in order to read?

- Decoding: sounding out words

- Vocabulary and comprehension of the English language

- Rules of the English language

- Memory and attention

? What if my child is having trouble sounding out the words?

- Read the word slowly and stretch out the middle sound, e.g., c-aaaaa-t. Have your child try the sound with you. Then have your child try again on their own.

- If your child is still struggling, I highly encourage you to go back to the Orange Books and build words. This revisit to practice building words will help your child hear the first, middle, and ending sounds of words.

- Remember, children often forget how to do something new, and your child may take anywhere from one week to one month to master reading the words with ease.

? What should I do if my child can't read words in a row?

Have your child read one word at a time while moving their finger under each letter. Then, read the sentence slowly while moving their finger under each word. Read the same sentence until your child can string the words together. The process is new and unfamiliar to your child. With practice, your child will read sentences.

FAQ

? What should I do if my child is having trouble focusing?

- TIME — Recognize your child may need breaks. Take a break after five minutes. Over time, slowly expand the time and the lesson.

- REPEAT — When you return, start at the beginning of the lesson — repeating something familiar builds confidence. Each time, your child will go further and further. When this lesson is easy, your child will be ready for the next challenge.

? Should my child practice writing as well as reading?

Yes! Reading and writing go hand in hand. To write a word, children have to *hear* it. Writing the words will help associate the sounds they hear with a letter. Words are made up of sounds that are written with letters.

? Should I stop to explain when my child asks a question?

If your child has any questions about English-language rules, feel free to explain them as you go along. For example: "Mommy, why does the word 'rats' have an 's' at the end?" "Well, when there is more than one rat, you add an 's' at the end."

? What if my child doesn't know the definition of a word?

Reading also requires comprehension, so to build your child's vocabulary, these books offer words your child may not be familiar with yet. Explain to your child the definitions of words as they come up.

? How can we integrate lessons into life?

- SENTENCE BOOKS — Children love reading about themselves. Write short sentences with your child's name, pet's name, friends, etc., and make personal books.

- DICTATION — When dictating, only use the sounds of the letters, e.g., "ck-ah-/t/" spells "cat." Use the word lists provided in the back of the book for dictation.

- EXTENSIONS — Help your child to further experience the concepts of the lessons. Have your child copy words and sentences they are learning from the book. Then have your child read them back to you. Practice makes permanent.

? Why do we only use lowercase letter sounds for dictation?

From a literacy perspective, to write and read, children need to learn the sounds letters make first. Once the phonetic reading skills are mastered, the names of letters are later used for spelling.

? What is dyslexia?

Dyslexia is the most common reason children struggle when learning to read. It manifests differently for every child and can range from mild to severe. At least ten percent of the population is dyslexic. This book is your tool to support your child; it is particularly effective in helping dyslexic children learn to read.

Review four and five-letter "a" words

crab

plan

camp

hand

plant

land

lamp

pants

scrap

sand

ramp

band

grass

glass

naps

jacks

scan

slam

hands

clam

clamp

snap

slap

stand

www.ingramcontent.com/pod-product-compliance
Lightning Source LLC
Chambersburg PA
CBHW041425090426
42741CB00002B/42